How to Run a

Business During a

Zombie Apocalypse

By Tara Richter

Published by Richter Publishing LLC
www.richterpublishing.com

Book Cover Design: Richter Publishing image from 123rf

Zombie images from Shutterstock

Editors: Haley Morton & Rebecca Nutting

ISBN-13: 978-1-954094-01-7 Paperback

DISCLAIMER

Dedication

I dedicate this book to all the essential workers who had to mask up and deal with the madness of the pandemic first-hand. Thank you so much for everything you all had to endure. Not everyone can work from home. We truly appreciate you being there for the rest of us.

Contents

Acknowledgments

I want to thank my clients/authors who stuck by our side during these difficult times. We truly appreciate your understanding.

I also want to thank Haley for enduring an internship that turned into part-time work during a pandemic.

To our future clients, thank you for your trust in your project. Every author we sign up keeps our doors open that much longer.

Warning!

This book is not meant for all business types. This is not a one-solution-fits-all guide. These are tips for some business models. You may not agree with all the tactics in here, and that's ok. The one thing the apocalypse has made us all realize is that someone is definitely going to be offended by this material. There will be crude and gross things as well. This is a zombie book. So, if you get offended easily, please give the book to someone else who will appreciate it. If you can think intelligently from multiple points of view and are open-minded, then proceed with caution. The zombies really like the smart ones.

Introduction

2020: the year of zombies, toilet-paper shortages and murder hornets. Who would have thought we would live to see *The Walking Dead* come to life? Not me. We are living in a real horror movie. And to top it off, some of us are trying to run a business during the most unprecedented times in our history. At this point in time, I have not found a book on how to run a business during a pandemic. (I'm sure many will come out soon.) Where are our guidelines? Where is our leadership! Most of us are running around like chickens with our heads cut off because the sky really is falling.

This book is my story of how I managed to keep my business afloat during the COVID-19 outbreak. On this emotional roaster coaster of riots and mask debates, it has not been an easy journey for any of us. Thankfully, my business is service-based and can be ran from anywhere in the world on Wi-Fi for the most part. I know not all businesses are the same. These are my tactics and the model that got me through it.

That isn't to say that I've been optimistic for this whole pandemic. At one point, I thought I would have to shut it down and walk away. Everything was overwhelming. In my head, I wrote the speech I would say to the authors, team members, to the world and everyone who has been a part of the company. I could never get through it all because I would start bawling my eyes out. Then I thought, *No*. I have worked too hard; I have busted my ass for almost 10 years now building this business. I'm not going to let a fricking virus come in and take me out overnight. There is no way I'm going out like that. Screw coronavirus!

At that point, I dug in deep and changed my mindset. I realized that the way I had been running my business since the start had already made it pandemic-proof. I had been getting so caught up emotionally in details and numbers that I lost sight of that. I only had to do a little tweaking to survive, because in 2020 it's about surviving, not thriving. It's not about comparing sales goals to last year, or any year for that matter. It's about getting through this shitshow and getting out on the other end okay.

That's what this book is: my tips and tricks to get through it. I include polled responses from other entrepreneurs about what they did as well — to show how they changed, moved and pivoted — as my business model may not work for all types of businesses, such as a restaurant or hair dresser. However, you might get some ideas and spark a new way of thinking for your industry.

I hope you enjoy this zombie apocalypse guide and I wish you the best of luck.

Tara Richter

So It Begins . . .
August 2019

I just came back from a four-month trip in Asia. I had lived in Thailand, Vietnam, Singapore and Japan. It was the most amazing experience of my life. I was with 17 strangers traveling and living in Asia. We had our own apartments, office spaces and were volunteering at nonprofits in each country. Most of us were entrepreneurs running our businesses while abroad. I have always been able to run my publishing house (based in Clearwater, FL) from anywhere there is Wi-Fi, but this was the first time I had put it to the ultimate test in eight years of business. Thankfully, it worked beautifully. Work during the day at the office, go volunteer at the elephant sanctuary in Chiang Mai on the weekend, eat pho on the busy streets of Hanoi for lunch and sing karaoke at the bar in Japan in the evenings.

I spent a week in Tokyo. It poured rain most of the time. That cold, wet, soaking-into-your-bones rain. I ended up getting pneumonia. I had never had pneumonia in my life. It was awful. I had a temp of 103 and had lost at least 15 pounds. This all happened days before I was supposed to fly back to Thailand. If anyone has spent time in Japan, you know it's really expensive, about the equivalent to living in NYC. So, I didn't have extra cash to go to the doctor there. Thankfully, a travel mate had some amoxicillin. I took that, and my fever broke and I felt good enough to fly to Thailand. As soon as I landed, I went to the pharmacist and got more amoxicillin for $5 and was good to go. I came back to the States in the beginning of August 2019. Lots of clients had waited until I came back from Asia to start working with me on their books — even though I could fully run my company and work with clients while overseas. My staff and I work and live remotely all over the world, so it really doesn't make a difference. However, some wanted to meet with me in person to sign the contracts and get started.

All of August, September and October of 2019, we were super slammed working with new authors. I hired a full-time admin, got a new office, and we were just humming away. Then came November. I got really sick; I had no idea what it was. I kept calling it the bubonic plague because all my symptoms kept changing. I was sick for two months and the doctors had no idea what was wrong with me — I didn't know what was wrong with me. Everybody I knew in Tampa Bay was sick during November and December 2019. We had absolutely no idea what was going on.

For me, it started out as an annoying dry cough. Nothing made it go away, not NyQuil, not cough drops, nothing. That lasted about two weeks. I went to the doctor, they said it was a sinus infection. I have had multiple sinus infections and it was NOT that! I had no symptoms in my sinuses, no runny nose or congestion. They gave me meds to make the dry cough go away. Those didn't help either; I just stopped taking them. At this point, I was exhausted for no reason at all. I thought I was just being lazy. So, I pushed myself too hard, being the Type-A personality that I am, laziness is not in my vocabulary. I swear I write books in my sleep. I pushed myself too hard and this mysterious illness went into my chest and compromised my left lung. I knew it was pneumonia because it was so similar to what I had in Tokyo. I was supposed to fly to Nebraska to spend Thanksgiving with my family. I told my mom I felt like death and went to the walk-in clinic the night before I was supposed to leave. I was sitting there waiting for my appointment for over two hours because there were so many people waiting to be seen. The ambulance came and took away an elderly man on a stretcher. I knew whatever this plague crap was, it was bad. I finally got in and the doctor diagnosed me with pneumonia, gave me an inhaler and the strongest antibiotic I've ever heard of. So strong that it can cause your Achilles tendon to rupture!

I canceled my flight for Thanksgiving. I went home, took my meds and still didn't feel any better. I seriously was down for the count until right before Christmas. I figured whatever this was, I just had to let it run its course. Thankfully, I'm 42 and healthy, with no underlying health conditions. The guy I was dating at the time had all the same symptoms as well. He was just two weeks ahead of me. He believes he got it from his six-year-old daughter, who probably picked it up from school. He was only in his 30s, so he never went to the doctor. Me being in my 40s, I went to the doctor twice; I wasn't taking chances. Right before Christmas, he texted me that he had coughed up a huge chunk of bloody mucus. I told him to go to the ER right away. Of course, he didn't. He was perfectly fine after that. All symptoms went away.

I finally started to perk back up in mid-December. I felt great for Christmas and New Year's Eve. The morning of January 1st, 2020 I started hacking something up. When you have pneumonia, the after-effects are coughing up all the mucus that your air sacs make to fight the infection. It's the worst part. I thought an alien was coming up my throat. My brother thought I was hungover from NYE and going to throw up. But I wasn't. I also thought all the remnants of pneumonia were gone. It had been over two months! I ran into the bathroom and then boom: a huge chunk of bloody mucus came out. I started to panic, until I remembered the exact same thing had happened to my boyfriend two weeks earlier.

Let the zombie apocalypse begin …

WTF IS Going On?

Jan.—Feb, 2020

After coming back from Asia and hustling hard, my company achieved the highest-grossing year ever in 2019. It felt good to start off the New Year after accomplishing great goals. I figured 2020 would surpass 2019, no problem. I was feeling great health-wise after being sick for so long. I had a new fire and energy inside of me. January was normal for us. Usually we're not super busy the first two weeks of January, plus we were working on taxes, getting all our finances ready. My admin was learning QuickBooks and doing a really great job. We were working in our new office and things started to pick up at the end of month like they normally do.

I had some new business deals in the works. I was preparing to launch an in-person training course for PR and how to land your own TV interviews. I was fleshing it out with a local TV anchor in Tampa. It was going to be an awesome new series. I was also scripting out a writing retreat to hold in Thailand in the fall of 2020. Lots of things in the works, lots of excitement.

I took a short vacation with a friend at the beginning of February to New York City. It was a great time in the Big Apple; we were totally oblivious to anything else going on in the world. When I got back to the office mid-February, watching the news was like, huh, wait, WTF is going on?! Someone ate a bat in Wuhan and now all of China is on lockdown. Thoughts raced through my mind: OMG I was just in Asia, wait, but I wasn't in China. But I was sick in Tokyo, but it didn't sound like the symptoms. Nope, that was just regular pneumonia. Wait … it sounds like EXACTLY what I went through in November of 2019. OMG. Where the hell did I get it?

Where's the Toilet Paper?!

Then on top of all this crazy pandemic news my admin sends me an email telling me that she's quitting. Really? I just paid her to get certified in QuickBooks and we are not done with taxes yet! More panic sets in. OMG, I need to hire another admin ASAP. Then I realized I had a new intern from USF starting soon, and I thought, *Let's wait on that for just a bit.* Thank goodness I did, because I had no idea what the future held.

I kept myself busy working on my new business deals. Then the TV anchor dropped off the face of the planet and stopped returning my emails right in the middle of fleshing out the new series. Ummm ok … that's weird. Authors started to back out of signing contracts. Hmmm … that's funny. Normally, by the end of February, we are slammed. Business started to slow down for no reason. I really don't watch the news much. Too much negativity. I stay in my happy, motivation bubble to get through the day. But my office grew eerily quiet literally overnight.

I went grocery shopping and there was no toilet paper. Cleaning products gone, hand sanitizer nowhere to be found. WTF is going on? Usually the shelves look like this right before a hurricane is going to hit the Florida coast. I thought to myself, *It's the end of February. It's not hurricane season?*

It started to sink in. This is bad. This is really, really bad. I started watching the news and reading all the crazy posts on Facebook. I seriously started to panic. I watched the movie *Contagion*. That probably didn't help! I started buying food in bulk from Amazon: cans of black beans, five pounds of oatmeal, ten-pound bag of brown rice, cat food and litter. My dad tried giving me liters of water; it's a pandemic, not a hurricane! But it was a nice gesture. I prepared for a month of isolation.

By the end of the month, the governors start talking about lockdowns. But I still had my office. CRAP, that's $650 a month. Business had already seen a nosedive and if we go into lockdown, what's the point of having an office that I'm paying for but cannot use? I have gone through this scenario more than just once. Should

I have an office, should I not? I know I do not need one because of the remote nature of my work. However, people have always guilt-tripped me into it. All the talk of "You're not a real company if you don't have an office. Where do I meet you? I need to come in and see all of you to make sure you are real. I want to go over every single edit in person with your entire staff." *Face-palm*. Now I was debating if I keep my office and ride it out, or just bounce all together. But we had more important stuff to worry about. Toilet paper!!

All jokes aside, I had bought toilet paper in bulk from Amazon months before the zombie apocalypse broke out. I was good.

Interns

The good news was I had my new intern starting. I really had no idea how I was going to show her the inner workings of a publishing house with a looming global pandemic brewing. She came into the office one time. I honestly don't even remember the conversation we had at that time. There was too much going on in the outside world to make this a positive, normal internship experience. Normally, I would have had training and hours in the office with a more structured format. But, with my admin gone, which turned into a blessing, I was just kind of lost in my mind of "What if" scenarios. After that initial day in the office, the next week I spoke to her and said that with the pandemic at hand, we were just going to work remotely until further notice. It ended up being the best decision ever, and worked out really well. And she has done an amazing job through everything in this weird environment.

I love working with interns. I never had the opportunity to be an intern when I was in college. I received my degree in Electronic Imaging & Graphic Design in Nebraska. They did not have internship programs at my university back in 1998. I went out on my own and visited companies, practically begging them to let me work for them for free. No one would let me. It was so depressing.

My company has now sponsored at least 50 internships throughout the Tampa Bay area. I really do enjoy mentoring college students and showing them what the business world is like, because it is totally different than taking classes. Some students even get real-world skills. I do not have children, so in a way I feel I am helping more people become well-rounded adults.

I've had some pushback about the internships being unpaid, however what the interns get in return is priceless. We normally utilize editors with English degrees or college seniors who are using the hours for graduation. They get to work inside a publishing house and we actually put them to work editing manuscripts. Once, an intern thought she was just going to be serving me coffee! Anyone around me knows, if you are in my presence, your butt is going to get to work. However, for every manuscript or project they work on, they get credit printed in that book. One semester I had three interns who each left with their names in 11 books! We give them print copies of each of the books they work on after publication. It's a win-win situation. Can you imagine graduating college and walking into an interview carrying 11 books with your name printed in them?

After running businesses in Florida for about 15 years, the one thing that is the biggest problem is finding and keeping good staff. It is a continuous problem. You hire someone you think is going to be a great fit, you spend the time and money training them to either discover they lied on their resume and really do not have the skills to succeed, or they leave. When you are a small business, one rogue employee can take you out. And sometimes you find amazing people out of the blue. About three years into business, I discovered an amazing girl who I hired as my first personal assistant once my publishing house was picking up the pace and I couldn't do everything myself anymore. I actually found her on Craigslist. She was looking for something different to do in between graduating from college and waiting to get into med school. She worked for me for almost two years, and was an absolute blessing. So smart and fun, she could have run my company without me. I knew eventually she would leave, but when she did, it was still emotional for me as I had grown attached to her like a younger sibling. I literally was in tears when she told me she finally got into med school — not tears of joy, which was selfish of me. But where am I ever going to find another one just like her?

In my emotional state of *What am I going to do now?*, I panicked and hired the next warm body that seemed "ok." Unfortunately, she lied on her resume and it took me awhile to figure out that she had no idea what she was doing. I also paid her way too much money. That was a hard lesson to learn. As I was training her, I was still doing my own job, plus her job and paying her. Eight months in, my company's profits went out the window. It was the first time my expenses were more than my profits. I have always run my business on a cash model: if I don't have the money, I don't do it. But she literally was doing nothing. She couldn't figure out how to publish a Kindle book after eight months. It's seriously not that hard. I was working 80 hours a week to pick up her slack, and traveling a ton. When my bank account dipped so low that I couldn't pay out the monthly expenses, I had to fire her. It took me three months of working alone all day and night to crank out the books I had in the pipeline with only one editor, because that's all I could afford. That one bad employee almost bankrupt me. I practically locked myself in a cave for three months working tirelessly to turn my company around. Thankfully, I can do almost everything myself to get the books published. That's how I built it, around my skillset. So, if I'm broke, I do the work myself. When I'm profiting like I should, then I can start subbing work out. This ended up being a huge money saver during the zombie apocalypse.

After that very damaging experience, I decided I would not hire employees straight out until they proved they could do the job. I started having many requests for internships throughout the years. During the internships, I watched and saw how well they did. Because I can train most people to do the job, it's about the work ethic. That is something you cannot teach; it is ingrained in you as a person. Morals and ethics are what I'm looking for in great team members. If an intern did a great job, at the end of the internship, I would offer them a position. This has worked out very well. I will still sometimes hire an admin straight out if they have enough experience, but I am way stricter with my vetting process and I never hire when I feel emotional about a situation. It's kind of like dating, you never want to hire someone out of desperation.

Tips:

• Do you really need a full-blown office space? You can save time and money by utilizing virtual offices. Most virtual spaces are about $100 a month and you get a physical address not a P.O. Box. It's an inexpensive way to have the appearance of a big presence.

• Internships are a great way to help college students prepare for the future and vet employees before hiring them.

• Try to not get emotionally connected too much to your staff. Especially when you must make tough decisions when hiring or having to let them go for the betterment of the company.

Food for Thought:

On the next page, use this space to brainstorm ideas for your own business. What kind of creative office space can you come up with? Maybe an addition to your house with a separate entrance? That would also add value to the property.

Food for Thought

_____
_____
_____
_____
_____
_____
_____
_____
_____
_____
_____
_____
_____
_____
_____
_____
_____
_____
_____
_____
_____
_____
_____
_____
_____
_____
_____

It's Alive

March 2020

By the time March came around, I realized that this zombie apocalypse is real. And it was going to last a while and we were not going to get out of this anytime soon. That was when the rumors of lockdowns and shutting down businesses were actually starting to happen. I really thought that we would be under martial law like they did in some countries such as Vietnam, Thailand or Peru.

I still have friends in those countries from travels in 2019. So, I was keeping in touch with them to see what was going on across the world and through expat forums. I was literally preparing for the worst.

Now, business had come to a dead halt. Which was understandable. Everyone was in panic mode. Writing a book at this point in time was not at the top of people's to-do lists. At this point, my entire goal was to cut all unnecessary costs. I just needed to batten down the hatches and save all the money that I could and not spend anything unnecessary. Money was not coming in, other than some royalties from books and payment plans I had other authors on from the previous year. But I had no new clients. No one was buying books, no one was going to be doing book signings. All events were being canceled.

One of the biggest expenses I had at that time was my office space. When I signed the new lease after coming back from Asia, I made sure the lease was flexible with a 30-day notice to leave. At that time, I did not want to be committed for even a year. Which is unusual for commercial leases, but I was just renting an office in a suite environment. In the back of my mind, just in case something happened and I needed to move, I wanted that option. Of course, I had no idea how important that would be in 2020. I asked the realtor three different times, "Are you sure I can opt out at any time?" That clause saved my butt $5,200. When March came and I gave my notice to vacate, the realtor said the pandemic would be over by May 2020 and that I should stay. "This is all going to blow over soon," he said rudely. Now here we are in October 2020 (as I'm writing this) and we are nowhere even close to being back to normal. So glad I bounced when I did.

I moved out of my office at the end of March. Shoved all my office equipment in my condo. Set up my new virtual office in my spare bedroom. I was actually happy, optimistic and in a positive mood. Not having to be in the office all day long: this is what I have wanted since I started my company eight years ago! I have always been able to run my company on Wi-Fi. I got this!

Now that I was all set up and ready to go, I stared cutting more expenses. Anything and everything I didn't need anymore. I wrote down a list of all my monthly payments for the business and personal, then decided what could go. I had a virtual secretary that would answer the phones, nicked them; that saved another $150 a month. Anything that was extra I canceled, even if it was only $10 a month. I kept only the absolute necessities. You know, like Amazon Prime and Netflix.

As I stated prior, my admin quit and that was a huge blessing in disguise. I didn't have 40 hours of work anymore to keep her occupied. Hell, I barely had 10 hours of work. We had some books still in the pipeline. However, authors were not working on edits or their books at all. So, everything just came to a grinding halt overnight. I'm also happy I learned my lesson about hiring in a panic mode. Because that was my initial knee-jerk reaction when she quit. However, I remember what happened in the past and decided I was going to wait a bit before I placed new job ads out. Now its seven months later and I still do not have a need for a fulltime admin.

Also during the downtime I figured out how to do other things like create our own ebooks on my new MAC. I upgraded my computer during Christmas sales and it paid off in more ways than one. So I was saving money everywhere.

Freelancers

Since day one of opening up my business, I have used freelancers. My normal office environment would contain a full-time admin, some interns, and then freelancers for everything else. Freelancers are a benefit in many ways. First of all, they do not take up physical space. Hence, keeping overhead down with smaller or virtual offices. Secondly, you can hire them for just certain projects. So if I'm working on a legal book, I can find a retired attorney to help me edit because they know the legal terms. This is really great to be able to flex the type of talent you have. If they do not work out well on a project, then you do not have to go through the hassle of firing or completing all the appropriate paperwork and possible unemployment costs. You do, however, need to make sure you have them sign independent contractor contracts with you, so you do not get into trouble.

Utilizing freelancers is a great way to be able to grow your business very quickly, or downsize it in case of a zombie apocalypse. Or even the holidays. For example, my business is slow during the holidays. So instead of having office space with employees sitting there bored, paying them to do nothing but play on Facebook, I downsize at those times. When the pipeline gets full and we are busy again, I beef up the team. Being able to quickly expand or trim down, this was another aspect that literally kept my business afloat during the pandemic. If I was stuck in a long-term lease with full-time employees, I would have gone bankrupt within three to four months after lockdown, if not sooner.

Tips:

• If you have an office, make sure to add a 30-day notice move-out clause.

• Utilize freelancers to easily expand or downsize at any point in your business. I prefer the site UpWork: https://www.upwork.com/

• Cut any and all excess expenses ASAP. Especially monthly memberships you don't use.

• For marketing use free platforms such as social media and listing sites as Yelp, Google Maps & Yellow pages online.

Food for Thought:

The best free marketing tool is Google Maps. I cannot believe how many people do not have their company listed there. I get inquires daily purely from that listing alone. How much are your monthly bills? Use this space to write down all your monthly expenses. Sometimes we don't even realize how much is auto-debited from our accounts until you add it all up!

Food for Thought

Will work
for toilet
paper.

Lockdown

April 2020

By April, most of the world was in lockdown. Different parts of the world handled it differently, including America. Our current Trump administration decided to let each individual state handle it on their own, and then each county did as well. So, it was very confusing to understand what the pandemic rules were. Since I live in the Tampa Bay Area, we have multiple counties you can easily drive across and not even know you are in a different zone with different rules. Tampa's newly elected mayor, Jane Castor, took a much stricter approach by installing curfews and more regulations and violations for restaurants. I live in Clearwater, and our restrictions were much less severe. We never had a curfew. They just posted large yellow signs about socially distancing on every storefront and sent alerts to your cellphone 10 times a day. For most of the summer you could still eat at restaurants outside. Nobody really cares about us in Downtown Clearwater. Everyone kind of forgets we are here, because we are right in the middle of the epicenter of Scientology. So we had other types of zombies to worry about.

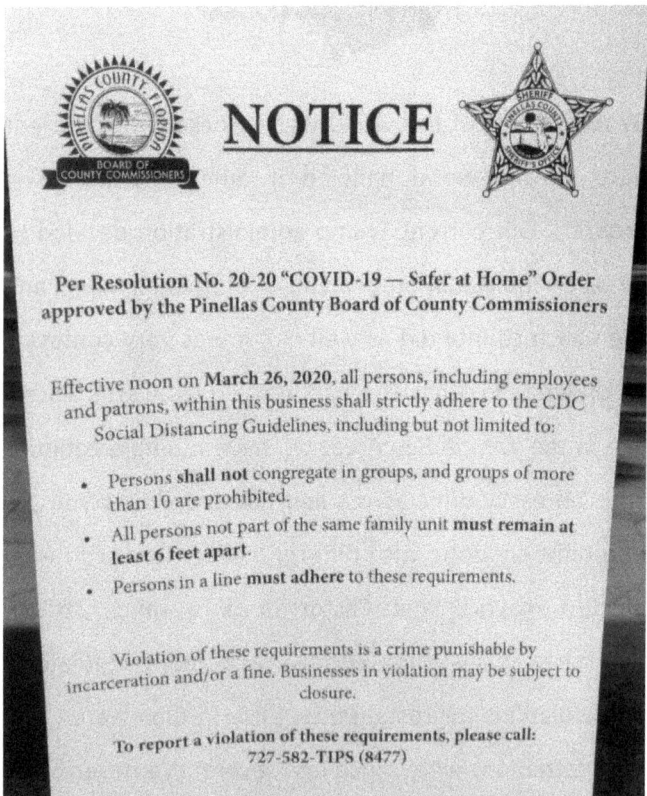

| T-Mobile 📶 | 6:46 PM | 27% |

Notification Center ⊗

Emergency Alerts ∧ Show less ⊗

⚠ EMERGENCY ALERTS — 10:05 AM

Emergency Alert
COVID19 If boating No more than 10 ppl on brd No boats closer than 50ft pinellascounty.org

⚠ EMERGENCY ALERTS — Yesterday, 5:21 PM

Emergency Alert
COVID19 If boating No more than 10 ppl on brd No boats closer than 50ft pinellascounty.org

⚠ EMERGENCY ALERTS — Yesterday, 4:21 PM

Public Safety Alert
FL Surgeon Gen: Stay home if 65+ or have medical conditions. All follow social distancing.

⚠ EMERGENCY ALERTS — Fri 5:32 PM

Emergency Alert
Reminder Pinellas Safer at Home Order in effect to slow COVID19 spread pinellascounty.org

⚠ EMERGENCY ALERTS — Fri 3:44 PM

AMBER Alert
#FLAMBER Alrt, Hardee CO, Triniti & Tristin Rodriguez, LIC/LGHW24(FL) 07 Black Lincoln SUV

My team and I were working fine from home. The transition really didn't make much of a difference for us. However, my business was still slow as molasses at this point. I had not signed up any new authors at all. We had a few books in the pipeline, but current authors were too stressed out to work on edits, or even want to publish, because no one wanted to release a book during a pandemic. Which I understood, there were more important things going on.

So, I was trying to be creative and do anything to drum up business. I ran sales on our current books, did all kinds of promotions, but it didn't matter. Even our book sales tanked. You would think people would have had more time to read, but our sales showed a different story. Sales went into the dumpster for all books. Our biggest sales are usually from business owners doing keynote speaking engagements and that all went away overnight. So, I went from having five streams of income to almost zero. It was definitely a panicky spot to be in. I calculated how much my personal and business expenses were for every month, and how much money I had in the bank. I calculated that I would be broke by July 1st, 2020 if things didn't change.

It was a rollercoaster of emotions: trying to figure out what to do, how to revamp and how to get business in. So finally, I came up with the idea to hold a writing contest to drum up business. Because people *did* have the time to write. Normally, I would hold a writing contest around the time of our huge annual author award ceremony and book a gala in November at the end of the year. We would announce the winner after the awards and the author would get a free editing and publishing package. I figured it would be best to move it and call it the Quarantined Writing Contest.

This turned out to be the best and the worst idea ever. The good thing was that Channel 8 News picked up the story. I actually reached out to them because I was watching the news daily — everyone was, to keep up to date on the pandemic. I'm not a news person but these were unprecedented times, and I needed to become abreast of the situation because it seemed to change hourly. While flipping around to different news stations,

I noticed that Channel 8 News had a segment called "Something Good." So, every day during the sad day of craziness of 2020, reporter Lila Gross would cover local people doing good things. So, I thought, *Hey, this would be a great segment for them!*

Basically, I searched her on Google and found her Facebook page. I reached out to her, stating I own a local publishing house and was holding a Quarantined Writing Contest for people to submit their manuscripts to get their books published. I was actually surprised she messaged me back the same day. Side note: this is why I like reaching out to news reporters on FB, because you can see when they have read your messages, versus an email. Sometimes email addresses go into the spam folder, so you do not know if they ever received it.

She said she loved the idea, but was worried I didn't have enough footage for the segment, as the TV stations were not sending out crews to film anymore. Little did she know that I have a YouTube channel full of tons of camera footage. Film from all of our past author awards ceremonies, book signings and other author events. I have days of footage. So, I sent her my YouTube page and said that wasn't an issue. She loved it, said "Great!" and we scheduled the interview right away because the deadline of the contest was May 1st to submit the manuscripts, and we were almost two weeks out.

So, we did our interview over Zoom, which was amazing. I have done many TV and radio interviews over the years. Usually it takes up most of your day. Because you have to get ready, do your hair and makeup, buy a new outfit. Then drive all the way there in traffic. Sit in the green room and wait for hours to do your five-minute segment. Then drive all the way home. So, this was beautiful. I already had all the equipment at home to do a professional interview, because of all the YouTube videos I record. So, if you do stuff at home, make sure you have professional lighting equipment. I got two standup LED lights from Amazon for about $150 and they have been worth every penny. Having proper lightening makes a big difference so you do not look like you are in a creepy basement. I know all of you have seen those awful interviews since everyone is broadcasting from home.

You want to make sure you have a nice spot set everything up. You don't want a pile of dirty laundry behind you. And make sure your pets and/or kids are occupied or closed off in another room to avoid interruptions.

We did the interview and it turned out great! The only thing I didn't factor in was that they reserve the lower third of the screen during the TV segment to show names and info. I always prop up my laptop when recording so you don't get that up-your-nose look. However, I didn't think about the lower thirds, so it kind of cut into my chin. But that's ok, because most of it was clips of our awards anyway. It was so good that they made two different segments that ran throughout the day.

We received thousands and thousands of hits a day to the website, and we got tons of submissions. The phone was ringing off the hook. The emails were blowing up, and it was great. I was feeling happy and productive because I was busy again. However, busy work doesn't translate into productivity. Even though I know this, I got sucked into its dirty little game, because I just wanted to feel like we were operating at the same capacity as prior to the pandemic. However, what I ended up doing was just spinning my wheels and going nowhere.

So, the big problem was, I was busy with the wrong kind of clients. If you promote something for free, they always compartmentalize you as a free service. They don't associate you with spending money. So, lots of the submissions that I got were people who had submitted or talked to us previously, but couldn't pay our editing and publishing packages. So, a majority of the manuscripts were just bad, and I wasn't going to edit those for free because they weren't even good stories. It really just ended up drowning us in work that we weren't getting paid for. And that's just the worst busy to be: a nonproductive busy without making any money.

So, the contest ended up being the best and the worst decision. We did receive a lot of publicity from it, and that was really cool. Some people reached out to us and said, "Thank you for doing this. It's giving me hope and inspiration." So, that was really great. But then on the other hand, it also made people mad. The entire reason for the contest was to get publicity, but there could only be one winner. For all the ones who didn't win, we'd offer them the editing and publishing package at a discount. Usually in previous years, this strategy works out well. However, during a zombie apocalypse it did not.

I thought since we were reviewing all of these manuscript submissions, what we could do to help people was to send them a short synopsis of their story, and explain why it didn't win and what they could work on to improve it. And that was the worst idea ever. People were already on-edge, emotional basket cases. So, me coming in — even as professional to give them advice — just blew up in my face. I actually received my first bad review on Google because of it. Because people misinterpreted my good faith and thought they were going to get their manuscript edited for free! FREE!!!! Seriously? A professional editor charges thousands of dollars. We already busted our asses for free reading and evaluating the submissions, now you think we are going to edit it for free? Most of the manuscripts didn't win because the storyline was so bad, with such terrible spelling and grammar, that it would take intense edits to bring it to a better quality.

I have no idea why I said I was going to do that. Everyone was pissed off. They were in this state of anger and all kinds of crazy stuff with the lockdown. So, when I started emailing people, they fought back and basically ripped me a new one. I wasn't prepared for that. They did not want to have professional critiques. They were upset. They were yelling. They were pissed. At this point, I even had people call the office just to yell at me and make fun of my YouTube videos. It was insane. No one has tact anymore. Any manners during a zombie apocalypse just go out the window. I seriously stopped answering the office phone because I'm not going to take that kind of abuse. Here I am trying to help inspire people.

We did, however, get a few decent client consultations from it and I did sign one paying client. Even though I had already known him for a few years, something good did come from this. So, looking back it was successful. We signed the winner of course as well, but I always say, if I get one client from an event, it was a success. So, this was an equally successful and disastrous event.

Tips:

- Do not give away too much for free.
- Free clients will always compartmentalize you as a free service.
- You can get your own TV interviews by reaching out to reporters on social media.
- Watch different stations and research to see what segment your story would fit into.
- You can watch the interview on our YouTube channel here: https://tinyurl.com/RichterPublishing

Food for Thought:

What kind of story could get your company good exposure? Are you doing anything to help out during the pandemic? Watch your local TV stations and write down here what kind of segments they have and who the anchor is so you can look them up on social media later.

Food for Thought

Mania
May 2020

The month of May, for me, was pure manic mode. I had all the submissions from the writing contest, which gave us a ton of busy work, but no real money yet. I had two months left of reserves to pay bills. I had applied for the different grants, PPP (payment protection program) and other various things the government was offering. Yet nothing had come through. I did not apply for unemployment, even though they said they changed the terms so that self-employed people could qualify. As an entrepreneur, I really hate trying to get a hand-out. Plus, the systems were totally messed up and it was an absolute nightmare for the millions of people trying to get unemployment. One thing I hate more than anything is wasting time. I didn't want to sit on their phone helpline for hours, or submit applications over and over again to have the site reject me and crash. I'm a business owner; I solve problems!

So, I set out on my adventure to reinvent my business model. This crap was not going to destroy me! I was going to take out those negative zombies one at a time. I was actually very positive and motivated at this time. I went into full creative mode. I felt like how I was when I first started my company over eight years ago. Money wasn't coming in, yet you are building a product — being creative, thinking outside the box.

My first project was to take my in-person writing series and make it all digital, and set it up as a monthly fee system. All the content was going to be online videos with homework assignments to help the aspiring author write, edit, format, self-publish and market their books. It sounds genius, right? Everyone loved the idea when I pitched it. It was going to be a much more affordable new aspect of my business. Once all the classes are recorded and uploaded, it's an automated system that just runs on its own and makes millions. Easy, right?

Well, that didn't happen. I put in the hours and hours of making the videos and scripting out everything in a perfect system through Kajabi. If you don't know what Kajabi is, it's a platform to create subscription-based biz models. What sucks though is that the minimum monthly payment is $150 to use their system. So, I'm paying money out while I'm creating this and at this point, $150 is a lot of money going out if nothing is coming in. We needed to cut all unnecessary expenses, not add them. But this was a calculated risk. If I got the thousands of users I thought would all jump on the opportunity to pay for my 20 years of experience in the publishing industry, it was worth it.

I was super excited and optimistic, as all entrepreneurs are. But as soon as I launched it, everyone who said they were going to sign up didn't. Why — I don't even know. For some, they didn't or couldn't part with the $20 a month, others I think were just too lazy. So, I spent hours and hours for only one person to sign up. I eventually shut that down because it didn't make sense. I did move it to a free platform after that fact, but it's not as nice as Kajabi.

As the problem-solver I am, I went around in my head trying to figure out how to make money. I tried everything: live Zoom classes. One person signed up, zero showed up. Consultation sessions, manuscript review fees, à la carte services, I had even been working on licensing models. Nothing worked. Zip, zilch, nada.

The only thing that did work was my original business model I had been using since the beginning. I drove myself crazy tying to reinvent the wheel that already worked. I eventually signed a new client at the end of May, but I had to slash my prices 50%. So in reality, I never really had to change a thing other than make it a bit more affordable because of the pandemic.

Zoom

Many businesses at this point are going to Zoom to handle meetings online. Which I do think is a handy tool. However, they can be lengthy and time-consuming. People are packing their days with unnecessary Zoom stuff. I avoid them at all costs unless I have to, like for the tv interview or doing a book launch. Then Zoom works great, but not for every single meeting. If you can answer the questions through email or a phone call, do that instead. Because what is the point of working from home if you are going to see me? I don't want to do my hair and make-up when I'm only hanging out with my cat. I don't want to spend an hour getting ready for a 30-minute Zoom call. I think they are a waste of time, like all meetings. People get stuck in being busy and not being productive. It is so much faster to send an email versus a phone call or a Zoom meeting. Especially for those that are not tech-savvy. You are going to spend 20 minutes just trying to get Karen set up with everything to even join in on the meeting. I'm so sick of people wanting to Zoom for everything. Zoom for happy hour, Zoom for meetings, Zoom for workouts. Blah, Blah ... NO! I only did three videos chats in eight months.

Tips:

- Don't reinvent the wheel.
- If your model works, stick to it.
- Do you really need to do a Zoom meeting for everything? Emails are much faster to answer questions.
- Being busy doesn't mean you are productive or doing money-making tasks.

Food for Thought:

Always do money making tasks first! I keep a list of things to do in my CRM system so every morning when I log on I see what is on my to-do list. However, I prioritize the money making ones. Then I delegate the other work tasks to the team. Write down what are money making tasks versus busy work.

Food for Thought

_____
_____
_____
_____
_____
_____
_____
_____
_____
_____
_____
_____
_____
_____
_____
_____
_____
_____
_____
_____
_____
_____
_____
_____
_____
_____
_____

Downward Spiral

June 2020

Now we had been in Quarantine for about three months. Businesses were not supposed to be open. Restaurants could only do delivery, no inside eating. Florida, at this point, had not implemented the wearing of face masks. Some people were, but not many to be honest. Bars were shut down. COVID cases were spiking; numbers for the US were not looking good.

June was a very emotional month for me because it was the last month of the automatic payments that I personally financed from the year before. And money was getting thin. I didn't know what I was going to do. I was frantically slashing my prices, trying to get anyone to sign up. I was still doing lots of phone consultations because people were interested in publishing, but no one had the money to sign up. Or the ones who did have the money didn't want to part with it. Authors didn't know it, but every client I did sign up at this point was literally saving my business.

I also was having difficulties paying out royalties, just because the monies from different distribution channels come in at various times. Money comes in and money goes out to pay bills and expenses, and just because we were in a pandemic, doesn't mean that I didn't still have all the expenses to pay. Thankfully, I downsized as much as I could, but shit was getting sparse. Way too close for comfort. At this point I was sending out royalties monthly. And that is a lot of work to download reports from multiple distribution channels all over the world and parse them out for 100 different titles in various formats. It's a two- to three- month process. Then having to email them to the clients and then cut the checks. I'm literally spending money to have a team member figure out how much money we have to pay out. So, I had to make the tough decision to switch to a quarterly payment system so it would not be as much work monthly, and so I could hold off on paying out monies I didn't have.

Of course, some authors were totally pissed off about this decision. One even blasted me on Facebook and tagged me in the post. Real standup guy. Here we are in the middle of a zombie apocalypse, I'm about to lose my business, everything I worked so hard for, and he's blasting me over a $200 check. However, it turned out to be the best thing ever. Because I told the authors that if they wanted to leave the publishing house at this point, I would give them their files and they could walk. So, it did a great service to me and weeded out the total assholes. They never respected us or all the sweat and toil we did for them. So, this was a great time to send them packing so they could do it themselves.

After that crazy incident, it made me refocus to no longer going to work with clients that suck the soul from me and disrespect my team members. Life is too short. I will not sell myself to the devil. No amount of money is worth it. I made the decision right then and there. I will only work with clients when we have a mutual respect, and they appreciate what my company has to offer. There are amazing clients out there. You just have to make room for them by removing the infection first.

So, I was moving forward in some aspects, but was also trying to keep myself busy. Being bored is not in my vocabulary. I also had a routine which kept me motivated for a while. I live in a high-rise condo so I have a pool and a gym. So I was great as long as I had my daily schedule; get up, coffee, gym, pool, and then work. This kept me sane for a bit until Pinellas County decided to shut down all gym and pools. This really just messed up my motivation all together. I started biking outside and walking but it was getting too hot in Florida

So with no new business going on, my routine screwed, it ends up in afternoons of drinking of wine, watching way too much Netflix and ordering too much pizza. I was back and forth mentally of Yeah, we're going to be a healthy quarantined person and lose weight during this. Woohoo! Then something bad would happen and just throw me off the cliff emotionally, and I was eating chocolate and pizza and I was like, "F everything."

PINELLAS COUNTY BOARD OF COUNTY COMMISSIONERS

PINELLAS COUNTY SHERIFF'S OFFICE

RE: All Pinellas County Hotels/Motels and **Condominiums** with Swimming Pools

Pursuant to Pinellas County Resolution No. 20-20: "COVID-19 - SAFER AT HOME" ORDER (Order), effective Thursday, March 26, 2020 at 12:00 PM ET, all **swimming pools** located at hotels, motels, lodging establishments, **condominiums** and commercial business establishments as well as homeowners associations shall be closed. This Order is necessary to enforce Centers for Disease Control (CDC) social distancing and group gathering guidelines. Pinellas County guidance on this closure reads:

"Places of public and private assembly **are required to close**, whether indoors or outdoors. This includes locations with amusement rides, water parks, pools (except for those in single-family homes), zoos, museums, movie and other theaters, public playgrounds, bowling alleys, pool halls, concert and music halls, country clubs, social clubs and fraternal organizations."

Pinellas County issued the Order to preserve the health, safety, and welfare of our residents and to preserve the ability of our healthcare system to serve all in need. Our emergency management and public health officials believe that the situation will quickly worsen without this intervention. It is our hope that following these measures will allow everyone to resume normal business operations sooner rather than later.

The requirements of this Order have the force of law and may be enforced by any available legal process up to and including being punishable as a crime by incarceration and/or a fine. To report a violation or ask questions about these requirements, please call 727-582-TIPS (84 77).

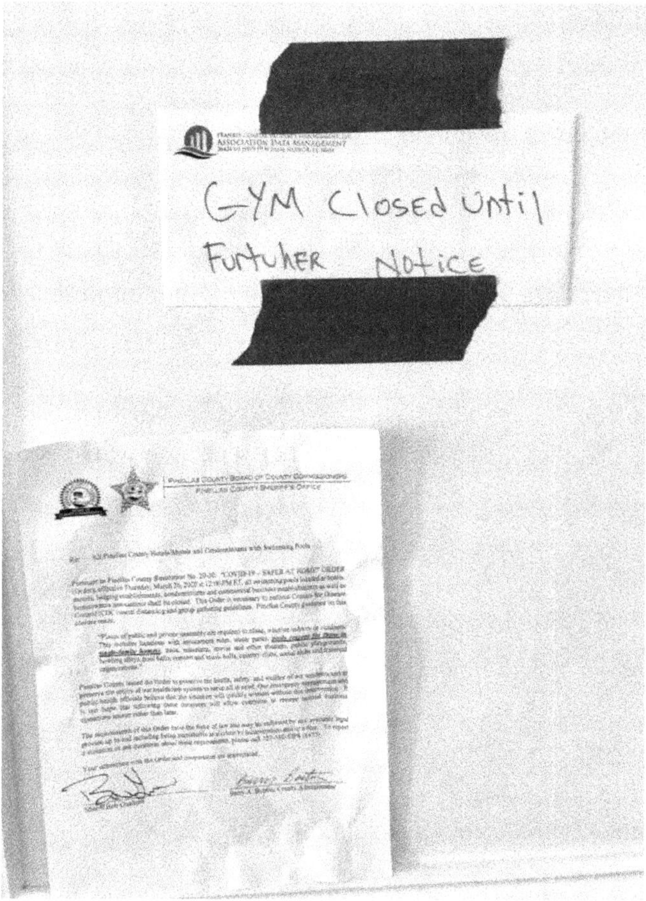
GYM Closed until
Furtuher Notice

I was to the point where I thought, *I'm just going to have to shut my company down and call it quits. If I don't have the money to pay royalties, then that's it. My days are done as a publisher.*

Some days I would just cry, sit at my computer desk and bawl, not knowing what to do. It took me eight years to build this business. All the blood, the sweat and toil, killing myself working 100 hours a week, networking my ass off. Doing so much for my authors and for this company to just have a zombie apocalypse come in overnight, just wipe it out. Then on top of that, having asshole authors demonizing me. It was so frustrating. I did not want to let my clients down. I also have a hard time sharing this openly with anyone, because we as entrepreneurs are just supposed to figure it out.

I'm the rock for everyone. My authors, team members, interns, family, when do I ever get a shoulder to cry on? When is it my time to ask for help?

I was coming up with worst-case scenarios. I could sell my condo and my Cadillac, make some money off that to keep the business afloat. Then I could move in with my dad until things picked back up. It was really bottom-of-the-barrel scenarios. So many ups and downs, trying to figure out what the hell I was going to do with my life, my business, my clients. Where was the money going to come from?

Usually in order to make more money, I would just hustle harder, go to more networking events. But this was different. This was a pandemic. It didn't matter what I did. Nothing worked because most of us had never lived during a global pandemic. People don't care about writing a book, they only care about staying alive and healthy.

Right when I was at my lowest moment, I finally got an email from the SBA, Small Business Administration, saying that I had been approved for a loan! I honestly thought it was some Nigerian scam email at first. I had applied for so much stuff months ago and no communication at all. I was freaking out, you've got to be kidding me?! It wasn't the PPP that was forgiven, it was just a straight-up loan that you had to pay back. I forwarded the details to my father to review to make sure it was legit. We both worked in the banking and mortgage industry for a while in the past. But yes, thankfully, it was legit! It wasn't a ton of money and I still have to pay it back, but with a very low interest rate of 3% on a 30-year fixed. OMG, this was my saving grace.

But I had to approve it first, then verify it was me and they said the money would just be deposited into my business account on file. Of course, they gave me no more details, like how long it would take. But at least I knew the money was coming. And because I had switched to a quarterly royalty payment, that gave me time to receive the funds. Fingers crossed. But who knows, maybe it would be another two months to receive the funds. Thankfully, it only took about three days!

Holy crap, I was going to be okay. I was going to survive.

Tips:

- Get rid of the zombie clients that infect your business.
- No amount of money is worth working with evil people, because they will stab you in the back as soon as they can.
- Only work with people you feel good about, because anything else is detrimental to your mental health.
- If clients owe you money and they won't pay, send them to a collections company. Some people will work with you, others need a 3rd party involved. I like https://rsgcollect.com/

Food for Thought:

Is there anyone in your company that needs to get the ax? Do it now. Don't wait. Write down the problem and how they make you feel. Do you get anxiety just hearing their name? Sometimes you don't realize how you feel about something until you get it out of your head and onto paper. Writing is very therapeutic.

Food for Thought

I'll Survive

July 2020

I finally got the SBA loan, which allowed me to relax and not be so stressed out. I'm a big believer that the energy you put out into the universe is what comes back to you. So, when you're in a lack state of mind, then you receive lack. And when you're in an abundance state of mind, you receive abundance. Now, obviously, this was still during a zombie apocalypse, so there was still a lot of stuff that was out of our control. I don't believe you can just sit on your couch and meditate, and money is going to fall in your lap. I mean, that would be great, right? *If* we could make that happen. I meditated with the Buddhist monks in Thailand and still don't have those kind of powers.

But I did receive the loan. And then almost immediately after that, I got two more clients to sign up. So once again, every client that signed up was literally keeping my doors open that much longer. I didn't tell them that, but that was the state I was in during the economic downturn with the zombie apocalypse going on. Things slowly started to look upwards.

I also started getting authors that had done previous books with us and wanted to publish a new book. Before, I was slashing my prices for new authors just trying to get any money in the door. Well, now I had previous authors coming to me that knew my price and knew that my company does a good job, and they had the budget for it. So, this was another thing that was keeping my doors open: having repeat clients.

Getting repeat business definitely is another great thing because you don't have to spend any marketing dollars to get it. They already know, like, and trust you, because they've already done business with you. So, this was a great thing to avoid having to slash my prices. I knew I was going to be good until the end of 2020 just with the three clients I had signed up and the loan.

Another important aspect in business is following up. It blows me away by the amount of professional people who do not follow up. The one author I signed from the writing contest was someone I met at a writing conference a few years back. But I always follow up with people. If someone has already expressed interested, I will send emails every now and then to see where they are at in their process until they say no or go another route. I also keep in contact with everyone I meet by sending out newsletters. I have retained clients because of our monthly emails. I try to not bombard people with a crazy amount of stuff, but I will send out notifications with our new books or events. Of course they can opt out, but by simply communicating in that way keeps you in their mind.

Mailchimp is a platform that now offers a free newsletter tool for up to 2,000 contacts. So I canceled my current software I was using that had gone up over the years to $30 a month. I trimmed my list down by weeding out the unsubscribed and dead emails to fit the limit. So that again saved me $360 a year.

I was finally able to relax. I wasn't as stressed out and enjoy some of the downtime. Even though we had books in the pipeline, I was used to normally working with 15 to 20 authors at once. During the zombie apocalypse, we only had maybe six at the most at one time.

I really started to enjoy not working like a madwoman 24/7. Again, being busy doesn't mean you're productive. I'm a type-A personality and I'm happy when I'm busy. So this forced me to really enjoy only working for three to four hours a day. I was able to go to the beach, ride my bike, meditate every day and take the opportunity to enjoy life.

I started to do fun things like document this pandemic with my new GoPro. I filmed everyday life and edited the videos and taught myself iMovie and other editing skills. I even flew back to Nebraska to visit my family at the end of June and made a little documentary about it.

That video has more hits on it than any video I've published to date.

The downtime gave me the space to allow myself to be. I think it would have been a little bit harder to do this if I hadn't lived in Asia in 2019. Those four months really made me revaluate my life and where I was headed with everything. Once I made myself a priority and not the business, I had a slight panic attack. Who am I without my publishing house? The company is my identity, we are the same. If I do not have this I don't even know how to exist in life.

Having that panic attack prepared me for 2020 and how to have a life separate from my business.

Tips:

• Repeat clients can help you keep your business afloat. Remember to follow up with older prospects.

• Meditate to help ease your mind.

• Enjoy the downtime.

• Self-hypnosis helps with mental blocks you might be experiencing.

• Deal with your anger in a safe way, versus taking it out on random strangers on social media.

• Take this time to learn new skills.

• Spend more time with animals instead of humans.

• See my zombie apocalypse videos on YouTube here: https://tinyurl.com/TaraRichter

Food for Thought:

How can you spend your time away from the zombie apocalypse? Take some time out for yourself. Reconnect with nature. Write down any hobbies you have always wanted to do, but didn't have the time for.

Food for Thought

Acceptance

August 2020

Come August, things were starting to open up. I believe at this point, restaurants could serve inside at a 50% capacity. In Florida, our numbers were going down and people were starting to go out more. They were starting to have talks of letting kids go back to school in the fall.

At this point in my business, I had some clients signed up and everything seemed to be okay. I got my finances under control, expenses under control, and honestly, I was good. I had come to the acceptance phase. We were not anywhere close to pulling in the amount of revenue we did in 2019. But that was ok. I stopped comparing my sales from 2020 during the zombie apocalypse to the prior years. You cannot compare the two at all; it makes no sense to. At the end of 2019, I had put my business up for sale, and of course gross and net revenue was all that anyone cared about. That stress of trying to meet the numbers is what caused me so much anxiety. But there was no way to even meet those goals and frankly, who cares? I didn't want to sell the business anymore; I don't have investors or a board to answer to. As long as we could pay the bills, it didn't matter.

With acceptance came peace of mind. Now I know I can still live comfortably, keep my business afloat and still publish books. Once I allowed myself to be happy with this, the bliss really came in. I honestly never want to go back to the crazy mania side of business. I like sleeping in, I like picking and choosing my clients, I like having time every day to meditate, do self-hypnosis and workout. It's really taken this pandemic to show me that it's not about the money. I don't need to be a millionaire. As long as I have enough to be cozy and comfortable, I can do this forever because now it's not consuming my life 1,000%. I'm a much happier, more relaxed person. I'm not strung out on no sleep and snapping at everyone. This is how life should be.

It's interesting isn't it? How it takes a global pandemic for people to realize they are not happy in their dead-end job. That they are miserable in their marriage. That they hate living in this state or that house. I see so many people making big changes and upheavals in their lives. And I think it's fantastic. Lockdown has forced people to be in their situation 24/7 without any escapes like work trips or outings with friends. It has made people focus on what is right in front of them, and they can no longer hide from it. I feel it's a great cleansing of the universal energy. Because people usually don't change when they are comfortable. They change when it's unbearable. So I do think that is a benefit we will all get out of this in the long run.

Now that I kind of fell into a cushy lifestyle business model, I've realized even more that I do not want people wasting my time if they are not an ideal client. Prior, when I had an office with a full-time admin, interns and more, I would allow any potential client to schedule a free 30-minute phone consultation. I have this awesome online scheduler tool where clients make their own appointments and fill out our forms. It's acuity scheduling and it's only $10 a month! (link will be at the end of this chapter.)

 It didn't matter to me if I was booked all day long because I felt productive and was sitting in the office supervising all the team members anyway. However, being busy is not productive, and all those phone calls did not flip into paying clients. It did, instead, take up lots of my time and energy giving out free advice to then have people go and self-publish.

This was something that had to go. I love helping people but I'm not a nonprofit, and my 20-some years of experience in the writing, publishing and print industry is worth a lot. Obviously, because people wanted me to consult them for free 24/7. Well I'm sorry, but that is not going to happen now. I don't want to be stuck in my home office giving people free advice when, instead, I could be at the beach or riding my bike or writing my own book like now. So the zombie apocalypse made me refocus and tighten up how I weed out potential authors.

Instead of letting just anybody schedule a phone call, I keep the link private and only give it out to qualified leads. So, my process goes like this:

1. They call the office and receive a prerecorded message that states we are working from home and not always available to answer the phone now.

A. If they are a signed client, then they can send us an email or post in their project management tool, Basecamp.

B. If they are a new author, they can go to our website and fill out our form.

2. We receive their emailed inquiry. From that information I can research who they are, what type of service they want and if we might be a good fit.

3. If they already have a written manuscript, we then send them the form to upload and they pay $50 for a review fee.

4. They now can schedule an appointment where we will review the manuscript, go over it with them during a phone call and give them advice of what needs to be changed or worked on.

5. If they sign up with us, then they have the fee credited back to their account.

6. If they self-publish, at least we got paid something for our time.

7. Most aspiring authors can be weeded out from emails, which doesn't take up much time.

8. If, at this point, the author does want to sign up with us, then we either do a phone call or meet at a coffee shop in person.

9. However, most clients we can sign contracts through Adobe Sign online and start editing online within our project management tool, Basecamp. We keep everything digital, so we do not have to ever meet in person if we don't want to.

Basically, I changed the weeding-out process so people have to jump through hoops. Editing and publishing a 50,000-word book takes time and effort. If an aspiring author cannot jump through these simple hoops in the beginning, they will never make it through an entire book project. So with this funnel, it's not even trying to weed out the people who have money and those who don't — even though that is important too — but it's seeing if these people can follow directions. Customers who cannot follow directions and want their hands held the entire time are the worst type of clients who will suck the soul from you. And when you have barely a breath left, they will take that from your lifeless body too.

Some people say that $50 is too cheap to review a manuscript and give feedback, and I will agree with those people. However, just making everybody pay a $50 review fee weeds out almost 90% of the tire kickers out there. If you cannot even part with $50 for a professional review from a publisher, then you can't afford the publishing fee. I have saved myself so many time-sucking, energy-draining calls by putting forth this small review fee. It's amazing really. People will throw away $200 on a fancy dinner, drinks and a night out, but will not invest $50 into their future. But that shows me they are not really serious.

So, once again, it's turning that potential author into a client that knows when they deal with us, it's a money transaction. That's also what went wrong with the free manuscript contest. I just got a slew of people who associated me and my company with "free" and didn't want to spend any money. By making everyone pay a $50 review fee, they're already in the mindset that they have to pay for my services.

I'm sure some of you are thinking I'm a publishing house so I shouldn't be charging for my services, but we are an indie publisher. We are not a traditional publishing house. When I first started writing my books over 10 years ago, I knew nothing of the publishing industry. I had worked in the presses but not actual publishing. When I started doing research about it, I didn't really like the model. All the authors I knew hated their publishers too, so I listened to what everyone said, and what I was going through as a new author, and basically flipped the traditional model upside down to start my company.

The way the publishing industry used to work was: you write a book, you find an agent, and that agent shops it to many big houses. You get turned down by many and maybe never ever get picked up. If you're lucky, you get picked up. However if they don't like the entire story, they might rip it apart, rewrite three chapters, and publish it. If you are lucky and they put any PR on it, you sell some copies, but they take 90% of the royalties and keep the copyright to your intellectual property. If they gave you an advance, you might not sell enough, and now they want some of that money back so they can cover costs. Anytime you write a new book, you are locked into a contract with them and they have first right for refusal. Sounds like fun, huh?!

With my model, the author pays us for our services to write, edit, format and publish on distribution channels all over the world. Since they pay us upfront, then we can pay our staff and give the author 80% of their royalties on the back end, plus they keep full rights to their work. Each contract is for individual titles; nobody's soul is sold to the devil.

So this is why it's important to weed out the qualified candidates who also understand the business model. How can you weed out clients and stop wasting time in your company?

TIPS

- Accept what you cannot change.

- Don't do busy work to just fill up time.

- Create a sales funnel that also weeds out clients who are just wasting your time.

- Spend quality time with ideal potential clients only.

- Utilize project management tools like Basecamp to keep everyone in contact at all times. And to keep you off the phone. Everything is documented in there to also cover your ass.

- Use a CRM (Customer Relations Management) system that allows you to track team members' emails and tasks so you can make sure they are really working from home. I like Less Annoying CRM:

www.lessannoyingcrm.com/invite/2512B

- Acuity scheduling system for phone calls:

https://acuityscheduling.com

- Decide what your long-term goals are. Is it more important to you to be super rich, or have a cushy lifestyle business?

Food for Thought

_____

_____

_____

_____

_____

_____

_____

_____

_____

_____

_____

_____

_____

_____

_____

_____

_____

_____

_____

_____

_____

_____

_____

_____

_____

_____

_____

_____

Sleep in & Shine
September 2020

Kids were back in school and everyone was freaking out about that on social media. Too much fighting was going on in the world. And me, what was I doing? I was embracing laziness.

I was personally giving myself a break. I don't care about business goals anymore. I wasn't trying to publish x amount of books. I was not trying to break goals, because that's ridiculous; you can't do that during a zombie apocalypse. And that's what was keeping me stressed out prior, was comparing where my business is at this year from last year. 2019 was our top-grossing year in the entire history of the company. But a pandemic is out of my control. I can only control what I do, and it doesn't matter. It doesn't matter as long as I'm surviving. It was not about thriving right then. I finally gave myself permission to embrace the laziness: eat the cake, order the pizza, have the wine and sleep in.

Back in March, I was trying to achieve all kinds of personal crazy goals, to lose weight and reinvent my business model. But now it's more about not being hard on myself. Just give yourself a break. This is a zombie apocalypse. Who cares if you gained some weight? Who cares if the house is a mess and your roots are three inches grown-out? The only thing we should all be doing right now is being nice to each other and to ourselves.

I actually started doing my own hair in January of 2020 and this also proved to be a helpful tool. And a creative outlet for myself to die it fun crazy colors. Before I felt I had to stay in the corporate look because of my clients, but hey, no more meetings and tradeshows! No one to impress. So not only was it fun to die my hair purple and pink, it also ended up saving me lots of money. Going to the salon is expensive and they were on lockdown for many months anyway. A trip to the hairdresser usually cost me around $350. I have a lot of hair. So doing it myself has saved me lots of time and money. I even watched a YouTube video on how to cut my hair and it wasn't scary at all! I don't know if I'll ever go back to a salon.

I'm a Virgo. I'm a type-A personality and most of my self-esteem comes from the goals I set and what I achieve. So allowing myself to embrace the laziness was not an easy task. This was work. I had to keep telling myself, "You know what? It's two o'clock. You can have that nap. It's 9 am. Go ahead, sleep in. You don't have to work out today. Go ahead, eat the cake, drink the wine!"

Who cares? Who are we trying to impress with our masks on anyway? I don't have any more red-carpet events. We don't have any keynote speaking engagements. We don't have any book signings. Those events were what always motivated me to get in shape in the past. I'm not saying to just let your health deteriorate, but you don't need to hold yourself or your company up to those high standards. Just allow yourself to relax, to be okay, to sleep in, to eat some greasy pizza, and watch Netflix.

I'm at the point of allowing myself to just be. I'm meditating every day, which I absolutely love. Sometimes I'll meditate twice a day. Sometimes I work all day. Sometimes I sleep in and I'll work for two hours, and then I go to the beach. I'm not being hard on myself, because we have too much going on in the world. Too much hate and anger and too many people dying unnecessarily. There's too much going on in the world to be hard on ourselves. We just need to all relax. It's going to be okay. We're going to get through this. We've had other pandemics in the world and the world has survived.

So many experts are all about "Rise and Grind" or 'The Early Bird Gets the Worm." Even before the pandemic I never fit into that 8-5 work mold. My circadian rhythms work differently. I used to be ashamed that I didn't like to get up at the butt crack of dawn and go network with people. But that is just not me. I'm 43 years old now, so I'm not changing anytime soon. I am not a morning person and I accept that. I am a night owl and that is when my creativity is the best and I thrive.

For me no matter when I go to sleep I have REM (rapid eye movement, which is the deep part of sleep) between 7am -10am. Not really the best time for me to get the deepest of sleep. However, that is my body and I cannot change it. Even when I lived in Asia for four months, it was only the first two weeks of the time difference that I was a morning person. For the first time in my life I jumped out of bed around 6am ready to take on the world with tons of energy. I was like, WOW this is what it's like to be a morning person! Woohoo! It only last two weeks and then slowly my normal sleep rhythms were adjusted and I was no longer a morning person.

So screw the rise and grind. So what if your rising is at 10AM? Does it really matter when you get the work done? We all have the same 24 hours in a day. My company has been very successful and I still sleep in and take naps. Sleeping that way just means I'm more productive the time I am awake. And that's what really matters. When I had a 8-5 job that cut right into my REM I was so messed up because I never got deep sleep. I was a walking zombie. I would force myself out of bed when I should be sleeping hard. Drive to work in rush hour traffic daze. Get to the office to drink tons of coffee that kept me up and attention for a few hours. Around lunch time I would fall asleep at my computer. So I built a fort in my car to try to take mid-day naps. It helped some, but basically I would drag myself through the day to get home and crash really hard for 2-3 hours then be up all night and repeat the cycle.

So having my own business definitely helped to create my own schedule. However, when you have an office full of people you don't want to stroll in at noon every day. Having everyone work from home was the best thing ever. And I schedule my client appointments when it works for me. Because I will never be a person who WANTS to be awake, social and talk to other humans at 7am EVER. And that's ok.

When I was married, I would sleep for four hours then be wide awake. During that time I worked part-time for a technology company from home, ran my own computer repair business and was taking classes to get my real estate license in Florida. So my sleeping schedule was midnight to 4am. Work from 4am to 8am. Go back to sleep and wake up to clock in at noon. Seems totally odd right? Well I found out many years later that it's called second sleep and many people used this two period sleep cycle throughout history.

Historian A. Roger Ekirch[10][11] has argued that before the Industrial Revolution, interrupted sleep was dominant in Western civilization. He draws evidence from more than 500 references to a segmented sleeping pattern in documents from the ancient, medieval, and modern world.[9] Other historians, such as Craig Koslofsky,[12] have endorsed Ekirch's analysis.

According to Ekirch's argument, adults typically slept in two distinct phases, bridged by an intervening period of wakefulness of approximately one hour.[11] This time was used to pray[13] and reflect,[14] and to interpret dreams, which were more vivid at that hour than upon waking in the morning. This was also a favorite time for scholars and poets to write uninterrupted, whereas still others visited neighbors, and did other activities. https://en.wikipedia.org/wiki/Biphasic_and_polyphasic _sleep

So, that's what I'm doing now, I am just accepting things and allowing myself to be okay, to relax and enjoy it. I am trying to plan new business events for the future. However, we don't really know what is going to happen. So I don't have deadlines for anything. When I was coming back from Asia, I was going to create a new business, which was going to involve writing retreats in Thailand. That obviously is not going to happen anytime soon. I still want to do that new business idea, but I don't know when. Probably not 2021. Maybe 2022. I don't know. I mean, there are so many unknowns. We don't know when we're going to be able to travel again. We don't know when borders are going to open up. We don't know when there's going to be a vaccine. So, I still like to plan and have my ideas, but it's an open-ended goal. It's just sometime in the future, I would like to do this.

Sometime, I will travel extensively again when borders open up, but I don't know when that's going to be and it's okay. I'm still doing my fun staycations, going to the different beaches, checking in on my father, or just jumping in the car and taking a drive. I live in Florida and the real-estate market is popping right now. People are tired of the pandemic and of being stuck inside up North, so they're moving to Florida. Interest rates are also at an all-time low. Right now (10/29/20) it's 2.5% on a 30 year fixed. Real estate is on fire! Now is a great time to buy if you need financing.

 A fun thing I like to do on the weekends is to go hit up open houses. It's fun; it's something different to do. You kind of have to think outside the box to keep yourself busy and happy. And I love house-hunting. It's one of my favorite pastimes, looking at real estate and doing some stuff like that just to keep myself occupied. And now I have the time to do it because I'm not working 100 hours a week. Now it's about reevaluating your expectations and what you want, because happiness is all about having the time to do the things you want.

Tips

- Be nice to yourself.
- Be nice to other people.
- Eat the cake, drink the wine.
- Reevaluate what you really want out of life and make those shifts.

Food for Thought;

What are your goals and aspirations for the future? Just because we are all on hold right now doesn't mean you have to just stay idle. Write down your future plans.

Food for Thought

Final Thoughts

I hope you enjoyed this guide to running your business during a zombie apocalypse. I know these tips do not adapt to all business types out there. A restaurant or bar is totally different than publishing books. But maybe it helped you come up with some new ideas for creative solutions in these unprecedented times.

I would also like to take a moment to recognize the number of small businesses who have had to shut their doors due to the pandemic. I have multiple friends who had to close down, and others I didn't know as well. It's always an emotional time when you have to throw in the towel and call it quits. I have run multiple small businesses and ending them never gets any easier, no matter what the situation is. This is something you have put your entire life into, and sometimes, all of your savings. I know why people cry on *Shark Tank*. It makes me cry watching those shows. Until you are an entrepreneur you do not know how much strength it takes to create and run your own company. We are the crazy ones, the lone wolves that will endure the shitshow because we believe in our idea. We push through after getting 100 no's. We are a special breed of people and not everyone gets us, and that's ok. I hate that this apocalypse has wiped out many awesome small businesses. However, I do know that we are resilient and for some, this might be the universe cleaning the slate to start over new.

Nobody has a manual for how to survive a zombie apocalypse — well, maybe some advice from bad movies — but remember, we are all trying to figure this out together. So, just be kind to yourself. Be kind to other people. Give yourself a break. Allow yourself to sleep in, drink that wine, eat that cake. And just enjoy the small things in life. Go outside for a walk. Start something new. Example, I hadn't ridden a bike in probably 20 years, and I went and got an old bike from my dad's garage and we spiffed it up, put some air in the tires and I started riding a bike again. I found HIIT workouts on YouTube to mix it up when it got too hot outside in the summer. I still want to travel and go hike mountains, so to condition myself for it, I started climbing the stairs in my condo. Do different, fun things to keep yourself occupied, like going to open houses. Or, just do whatever makes you happy. And allow yourself to be okay to have that downtime to not judge yourself harshly, and meditate. Meditate daily if you can to ease anxiety. I use videos on YouTube. I'll put some links here of the ones that I like. I like to put on a sleep hypnosis video for whatever I'm working on to improve myself at that time. And I will listen to it and fall asleep to it, and it gives you the best sleep. And sound therapy is really awesome too. The monks are really big into sound bowls, and I ended up buying a sound bowl when I was in Denver hiking in the mountains right before this zombie apocalypse broke out, and I absolutely love it. There are also sound healing videos online that are just amazing, and help to decompress the stress away. I like to listen to the videos daily. The list I created for you is here: https://tinyurl.com/TarasMeditation

I look forward to getting through the end of 2020 with you. Stay safe, my friends.

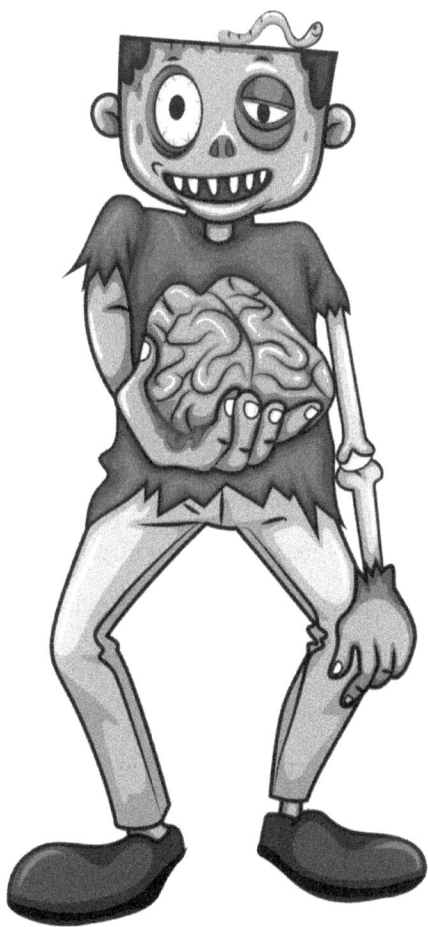

Advice from Other zombies

I asked other entrepreneurs on social media how they have changed and adapted to working during the pandemic. These are their responses:

Sarah E. Varughese, Photographer:

I took my pet T-Rex (named Martha), and turned her into the branding mascot for a new business — She-Rex Marketing Solutions. I've been a photographer for the last eight years, but all of my jobs started canceling or postponing. So I needed a way to still make a living. So I pivoted. I have a background in marketing and education. I've always wanted to do this kind of business; I just never had time to pursue it with how many photography jobs I normally have. I got the LLC approved in April (it took less than 24 hours to get approved). And I launched my beta programs in June. I'm now in the process of revamping the digital courses. But I've started private coaching sessions as well. It's been a great adventure! Even though my photography jobs are starting to pick back up again, I'll keep building up She-Rex until I can make a transition and swap it to the primary business. www.she-rex-marketing.com

Jana Grant, Realtor:

I took up painting again. Now I can sell that house and decorate it too! During the lockdown and subsequent spike, I had a COVID-19–positive client that wanted to see homes. I had to let her go to someone else because she wouldn't get a test to show she was negative. Also, I asked a realtor friend to do some referrals from my advertising. I'm now showing and listing homes again, but I bring masks and complimentary hand sanitizers for everyone. I took a small biz loan to stay afloat and traded my pricey car in and bought an older one for cash. I also refinanced my house in order to pay off all my outstanding debt. So much pivoting! It's the quick or the dead.

Christopher Timmons, Former Section Chief at 8 MXS
Egress Section Military, Now Lowes Employee:

From a business perspective of working in the retail environment, I have to say the key to success is flexibility. Bend, but don't break. If you have to spend a little extra on signage or protective stuff like masks and hand sanitizer ... DO IT. Your bottom line will be a lot worse if your workforce is in quarantine. Many dynamics have changed. Such as, break rooms can't be as full, so they need to stagger break times. Specifically in retail, you want to spread your people out more instead of concentrating and attacking a single aisle. Don't use COVID as a crutch to say, "We can't do that," but as an opportunity to be flexible and find a new way to get the job done.

Nathan Johnson, Web Designer:

I haven't gotten any sleep during the pandemic. We are busy getting everyone online with our award-winning websites and digital marketing.

www.allisonsalligator.com

Barbara LoFrisco, Therapist:

I embraced telehealth. I like telehealth for convenience and some people are comfier in their homes. But there can be a bit of a disconnect with the screen in between. Sessions seem to flow easier in person, easier to make a human connection. But I can see the benefits of telehealth more now that I was forced into it.

counselorbarb.com

Angye Smits Fox, Real Estate Broker:

As a real estate broker, virtual became our reality. Showing clients properties using a virtual tour became a necessary marketing tool.

www.adsizzlerealty.com

William McKissock, Expense Reduction Specialists:

I began interviewing local businesses and promoting them for free on social media during the lockdown, as my way of helping the community. Still doing it.

www.schooleymitchell.com/wmckissock

Ulunda Baker, East Region Sourcing Director JLL:

I've learned that it's not so bad working from home all the time, when you only have to worry about a nice dress shirt and not the pants. I've been living in my pajama bottoms on most work calls. My new motto is, Dressed up and pajamas down! These days I don't have to worry so much about my kids running around in the background or dogs barking while I'm on a call. Everyone on my team is in the same boat. The virtual working world has been the best place to bring your whole self to work! That's lifted a ton of pressure off of me being a working mom.

Nichole Clifton, Claims Adjuster:

Overplaying that you or your customer is a nurse, doctor or implying that they are more "essential" to attempt to sway the importance or need to expedite their claim is not well received. It has no effect on emotion and only makes the other person - who's also working during the apocalypse - feel that your entitled and downplaying their own "essential" status.

Here are the tips to survive a zombie apocalypse as images you can cut out and post in your office to keep visual reminders while you work!

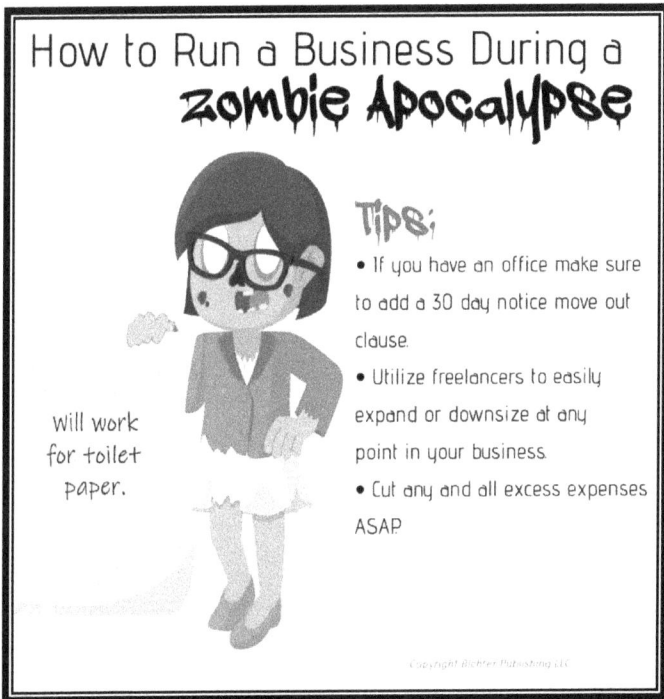

Tara Richter

How to Run a Business During a **Zombie Apocalypse**

TIPS:

• Get rid of the zombie clients that infect your business.

• No amount of money is worth working with evil people because they will stab you in the back as soon as they can.

• Only work with people you feel good about, Otherwise it will be detrimental to your mental health.

How to Run a Business During a
Zombie Apocalypse

Tips:

• Do you really need a full-blown office space? You can save time and money by utilizing virtual offices.

• Internships are a great way to help college students prepare for the future and vet employees before hiring them.

• Use online project management tools like Basecamp to keep everyone in contact 247..

Tara Richter

Tara Richter

How to Run a Business During a **Zombie Apocalypse**

Tips:

- Meditate to help ease your mind.
- Self-hypnosis helps with mental blocks you might be experiencing.
- Deal with your anger in a safe way versus taking it out on random strangers on social media.
- Enjoy the downtime.
- Take this time to learn new skills.
- Spend more time with animals instead of humans.

Tara Richter

How to Run a Business During a Zombie Apocalypse

TIPS:

- Be nice to yourself.
- Now is not the time to compare 2020 sales with any other year.
- It's about surviving not thriving.
- Eat the cake, drink the wine.
- Cut out unnecessary monthly memberships.
- Keep important ones likes Netflix & Amazon Prime.

ABOUT THE AUTHOR

Tara Richter is the President of Richter Publishing LLC. She specializes in helping business owners learn how to write their non-fiction story in four weeks and publish a book in order to become an expert in their industry. She has been featured on CNN, ABC, Daytime TV, FOX, SSN, Channel 10 News, USA TODAY, Beverly Hills Times and radio stations all over the world.

Her degree is in Graphic Design and she worked in the copy and print industry in the Silicon Valley. She has written and published 12 of her own books in just a few short years. Tara now has published many other authors all over the world including Anthony Amos and celebrity entrepreneur, Kevin Harrington, Shark from ABC's *Shark Tank* with their joint book, *How to Catch a Shark*.

The publishing house was not her first business though; she has been an entrepreneur her entire life and has opened multiple small businesses. One of which was a successful online computer repair company she operated from 2005 – 2010.

Tara also has a love for traveling and experiencing cultures all over the world. She can't wait for borders to open up again after this zombie apocalypse so she can continue country-hopping and volunteering at nonprofits like she did in 2019.

Connect with Tara on her websites & social media:
www.richterpublishing.com
www.tararichter.com
www.facebook.com/richterpublishingllc
www.twitter.com/tararrichter
@richterpublishing on Instagram
www.linkedin.com/in/tararaerichter
YouTube: https://tinyurl.com/RichterPublishingLLC

Find all of her books on Amazon:
http://www.amazon.com/Tara-Richter/e/B00CGKD8FG

Halloween is Tara's favorite holiday and she loves dressing up like zombies.

www.ingramcontent.com/pod-product-compliance
Lightning Source LLC
Chambersburg PA
CBHW060357090426
42734CB00011B/2162